Athazagoraphobia
(n) ~ An intense and persistent fear of being forgotten or of forgetting someone or something.

Athazagoraphobia

Chris the Poetic Genius Green

Wider Perspectives Publishing ¤ 2025 ¤ Hampton Roads, Va.

The poems and writings in this book are the creations and property of Chris Green - The Poetic Genius, the author is responsible for them as such. Wider Perspectives Publishing reserves 1st run rights to this material in this form, all rights revert to author upon delivery. Author reserves all rights thereafter: Do not reproduce without permission except Fair Use practices for approved promotion or educational purposes. Author may redistribute, whole or in part, at will, for example submission to anthologies or contests.

Cover art by Talis Matreshka

Editing Services provided by Crickyt J. Meyer

© 2025, Christopher Green, including writing as Chris Green and thePoeticGenius
1st run complete in January 2025
Wider Perspectives Publishing, Hampton Roads, Va.
ISBN 978-1-964531-99-1

Dedicated

to Robert E. Thompkins, Sr. & Donna Thompkins
(Grandpa and Grandma)
May you always live on in my memories.

Contents

I Time Is A Thief   1
The Plight of Being Human
Time Withers   Brittle

II Fighting For Memory   6
Fate of Forgetting
A Disguise of Myself   Cursed Inheritance
Hoarding Memories   Athazagoraphobia

III I Still Hear You   15
Memory Bank
Call to Remember   Distant Memory
Memory   Grandma's Lessons (for Grandma Donna)
Grandma's House

IV All Of Us Are Changed   25
Confirmation
Sieve   Lost   Vehicle for a Memory
Grandpa's Mind   Remembering Mortality

V To Live Beyond Death   38
Immortality
Content   Remember Me

1
time is a thief

The Plight of Being Human

Growing up, I carried an unearned angst about living- just a child carrying undeserved torment, blessed with a loving family, cursed with ungratefulness. I used to get mad and wish I was never born; tell anyone who would listen that it was unfair I was brought here with no choice in the matter. I was just a kid, with no real sense of what true pain was or what true torment felt like, a kid who hadn't experienced life yet.

When I became an adult, no matter what pain I went through, I never wanted to die. I feared death, even, and embraced being alive, although I had no say in my beginning. I finally decided to control the direction of my story.

I never seen my grandfather ungrateful, always saw him show gratitude - even when he was losing the ability to control his behavior. My grandfather and grandmother were the strongest people I knew, especially my grandmother. Grammie had a toughness, meanness (when needed), that remained unmatched all through her days.

Yet, there I stood, watching my grandpa forget himself and others, watching my grandma display heartbreaking physical pain; knowing not only is time undefeated, not only were my grandparents withering away, but that one day I would, too.

Time Withers

Time is a thief that moves while we sleep
We know not when it takes away
We pause for moments, we take breaks
But time just ticks away
It always moves but never leaves us
Still, we beg for it to stay
Time makes flowers out of us
Then watches as we wither away

Brittle

I haven't seen my grandparents in months.

Can't stand to see my grandma in pain.
She's always sick, and her bones ache.
My heart breaks
at the sight and sound of her agony,
when it's not an act.
Can't always tell;
she's a hypochondriac.
That's another subject, but can't discredit
the literal ache in her bones.
They're brittle
like the snack she used to love to eat,
but now doesn't have the power to in her teeth.
Another thing taken away.

My grandfather can't remember month, year, or day
and most of his memories have been stripped away.
His character being changed, his mind being hijacked;
Heard that earlier, he called my mother (his daughter)
his wife's name.
Asked her when they were going home.
My mind blown, his mind gone,
and I'm angry about it;.
breaks my heart at the same time.
That vile sickness, mind-thieving Alzheimer's
feasts on his memories,
chewing up and spitting out the best ones.
His once beautiful mind becoming a gutter.

I don't know what's going to happen when one loses the other...

I can't imagine if it's my grandfather first.
My grandma already lost her parents, her siblings, and one child.
I don't want her to bury the love of her life.
Sadly, maybe my grandfather will forget her eventually.
But that would be the last straw, mentally.

I guess I should be stronger, physically,
and visit more.
Been more coward than grandson,
avoiding the confrontation
with my fragile emotions
at the sight of their frail bodies
and sapped spirits
when I once marveled at their strength.

Stuck in my own mind wondering,
When did time come and steal our youth?
When did disease and fear break through our bonds?
Who will be there still, when the façade of my invincibility
is gone?

When my immortality fades,
succumbing to my old age,
a literal sick shell of who I used to be –

Will I be forgotten, like my grandfather's memories?
Will those that love me, still have the courage to face me?
Or, will those bonds, too, become brittle?

fighting for memory 2

Fate of Forgetting

From childhood to adulthood, we create memories. Some are long lasting and some fade with time. I never bothered to think of the ones I've lost. Guess I didn't remember to, but until now I never feared losing them either.

When your grandfather, his sister, and their mother lose the ability to retain memories, does it reveal a cursed inheritance? Will I suffer from such a fate of forgetting?

A Disguise of Myself

I often get accused of

Forgetting who I am

I wonder if that will ever be

A literal explanation

Who will see me trapped

Inside a disguise of myself

I just hope I'll always be

Remembered

Cursed Inheritance

Hoarding memory;
Chain Self to Identity,
So I don't get lost.

My Grandpa lost his mind.
Not like went crazy,
just had film erased from his highlight reel

I hope everyday not to become a sequel,
to not run out of footage.

When I remember what I'm supposed to,
my mind throws a celebration.
And, there's terror in that.

Haunted by spirits of memory loss:

My mind a time bomb,
how long before it explodes
thought into fragments?

Bits of cherished memory
scattered beyond reach, a forgotten wealth of love.

Disease the timer,
ticking through generations,
a silent death date.

The host, a hostage to self,
Death, the ransom note;
promised end to misery.

Cursed inheritance;
past lost, future blindsided
--just like grandfather.

Hoarding Memories

When statistics say that you'll lose the ability
to retain memories,
you tend to hoard them,
surround yourself with them.
– Even the ones you fought to get out,
thought you forgot,
until you smell the rot,
forced to live with it again.

Today, I noticed more often I smell rot
instead of flowers.
Not a side effect of COVID,
yet I'm still sick of it.
I fear the cost, my good memories lost.
Gamble with them on substances
which have no substance.
And wonder,
     ... if one day,
          I'll have no substance.

No matter how hard I try to secure myself,
trying to grow correctly into manhood –
having seen it, the destruction,
I try to embody the faith that the fate I think awaits,
is wrong,
that one day the weight of this fear will be gone.

I know I have courage to live.
'Cause Death gonna come anyway.

Was comfortable with it being any day,
but now I see it could be any moment,
so, visually take snapshots
of damn near everything.
So I don't forget...

Maybe I'm rambling...
I just hope when I'm gone,
I am not forgotten.

Athazagoraphobia

I often get accused of forgetting who I am.
Will it ever be a literal explanation?

When your grandfather and his sister and his mother
all lost their memory, you wonder
each passing year,
with each shortening of your short-term
if it's in your long term

If age is a conqueror, ready to wage war on the mind,
with no regard for love or family or connection,
Or if it's an intersection
with drunk driving thoughts
and under construction too often.

I think of its destruction too often.

When thoughts crash,
I stare at myself and ask,
Have you forgotten you?
Will you?

When time starts to wither you like an unnurtured rose,
after you bloom,
Will you be surrounded in a room full of flowers
you can't remember the scent of,
unable to make sense of your senses?

I'm told it's senseless to believe I'll forget me,
that I'll disappear in front of my eyes,
walking around with an expunging mind,
a betrayer of self.

Or worse, that I'll be forgotten,
no memorial of memory,
no second life (but the one that awaits me on the other side),
not alive on the tongue,
with no recount of my days,
That, to this world, I'll fade away;
a story unspoken, lost history,
Finished.
Erased.

3
I still hear you

Memory Bank

When you fear losing memory, you tend to hoard as many as you can-the good, the bad, and even the ugly. I find myself not wanting to forget the simplest things. When one escapes me, I wonder how many more fall through the cracks.

I surprise my loved ones, at times, going into the vault of memories and pulling out time stamps of our lives almost lost. I proudly go through my collection at family gatherings, running into old friends, campfires - like a historian, proud of his knowledge. I've remembered things my people aren't sure why I know, as if it were forgotten I was there. Memories of childhood my own mother didn't know I was alive for.

I keep those memories locked with a key and a pin, hoping my thoughts never break in and spend recklessly. I'm a recollection hoarder, hoping my memory bank is never empty..

Call to Remember

It's sort of strange,
how memory always calls to us.

Maybe it is as afraid of death
as we are.

Distant Memory

She said she looked forward
to creating more memories with me.

But that feels like a distant memory;

In between feeling forgotten
and wondering if she meant it

Or not.

Memory

Have you ever been afraid to create a memory?
Fear that you'd burn a bad one over top a good one?
Save over an important file with images
you never meant to keep?

I never wanted to see my grandma this way,

A woman with more often too much strength
feeling the strain of living.
Today, I feel the pain of remembering
her time is coming.
Hearing her oxygen tank by the clock ticking,
my head is spinning 'cause I'm digging
for better thoughts.

I know!
She's ready for Pop to pick her up...

I'm still remembering I didn't tell him enough
about how I feel,
and knowing I'm doing the same again,
feeling this pain again;
knowing at the sight of one of these suns
her light will go out.

I hate that I'll remember this darkness.

Don't wanna see her like this,
not to be heartless, but
Don't have the heart to burn the memory of her deathbed
in my head.

Burn time and regret instead.
Strengthen my avoidance.
Deny my acceptance.
Take my walk of shame while asking questions like,

Have you ever been afraid of creating a memory?

Grandma's Lessons
(for Grandma Donna)

My grandma won't the traditional grandma.
The first thing she ever taught me
was how to cuss.
Picking up her lingo when I could barely talk,
sitting round the grown folks, soaking up knowledge,
Momma scared what will fly out my mouth
whenever I spoke.

My grandma won't the traditional grandma.
Instead of cookies, cakes, or pies
drawing me to the kitchen,
it was fried chicken or rice pudding,
and both were legendary!
My grandma wasn't soft and sweet.
She was strong and scary;
told Los she'd beat the Devil out of him.
Made us and Hell tremble!

My grandma is sitting in glory
and I can still hear her yelling,
"Go out doze somewhere;
I'm trying to watch my stories!"
Though, she had more interesting ones than ABC.

My grandma didn't have boring old grandma stories.
She had ones not made for TV.
Her life was hard and it gave her the toughest shell
I've ever seen on a woman.

Built to survive
through the times you could still hear the slavery,
my grandma still wore some of those chains.

My grandma won't the traditional grandma.
Life didn't let her be.
I didn't need hugs and kisses and I Love Yous.
She loved me by helping to create everyone I love.
She loved me by putting food in my stomach,
smacking hard lessons upside my head with her mouth,
watching her trudge through life with a broken heart and body
and still be the glue holding us together,
– while her grief probably couldn't be fathomed.
By teaching me silent strength, even in crying times,
How to preserve through trying times,
How to keep going when you want to give up,
How to still look like the strongest person in the room
– when you're not,
How to never let anyone make me be silent,
How to be defiant, proud, and humble,
How when life takes your legs from you,
– still refuse to stumble,

And how when it's your time to leave this earth,
to lay your life in God's hands,
gentle and quiet,
'cause your life spoke loud enough.

Grandma, *you* spoke loud enough.
                And, I still *hear* you.

Grandma's House

I can hear the call from Grandma's kitchen
beckoning me for fried chicken.
Can hear her voice coming down the lane,
knowing the house is vacant now.
I can see my Pop waving at me from my steps,
wishing I knew how little time we had left
in those days.

Those days…
The house was a Sunday dinner away from Paradise.
Love filled every room, and soul food filled every belly.
That house was small, but fit every individual family;
a beautiful collection of all we are.

Me and my cousins filling the yard
with distractions from grown talk.
Playing kickball,
hoping not to hit a window.
Pop chasing us down the lane with his voice
when we do.
Playing hide and seek
or riding bikes,
and the invisible barrier in front of the street.
Stepping to the edge we weren't allowed to cross.

My grief signals I'm on the edge of memories
I shouldn't cross.

I miss my grandparents;
how they were the relics and glue,
pointing to a time long before me,
they way they held us together.

Now, they're still together,
but gone.

Mother's home our new gathering place,
Sitting at the Grown Folks Table –
My Uncle in Pop's seat,
My Aunt in Grandma's,
and their names ringing through conversations,
like legends.

Hard to find acceptance.
Hard to agree to the terms.
They had a contract to keep with God
and I never knew
they were approaching the deadline.

How my family is so close today is another memory
I'll have to fold up and tuck away in my mind
tor safe keeping,
hoping it is never as vacant
as Grandma's House.

all of us are changed

Confirmation

I used to wonder where the expression 'See the wheels turn in their head' came from. I didn't see wheels turning, but I saw my grandfather searching through muddy thoughts, attempting to relocate a specific sinking one until it was completely covered. My cousin had asked him questions about his mother. I guess, expecting to hear about a legendary family figure we never got to meet, but instead caused a confrontation with a type of pain I was unprepared for.

That day, I experienced the truth about my grandfather's disease. He used to tell me stories about my great grandmother and his childhood. Used to use her for lessons on how to treat my mother, but I could tell he had forgotten her. In that moment, I wondered;

Who would be forgotten next?

Sieve

Thoughts into fragments;
                a forgotten wealth of love
A silent death date;
                a promised end to misery

Family undone by the mind thief;
                … all of us are changed.

Lost

Can't remember how I conquered the fear of forgetting
Can't pinpoint the moment I let go of the thread
Or what cloth I'm cut from
What needled and stitched me into the man I am,
Living only in moments
Can't remember the memories framed or where I hung them
Stranger in my own head
Long ran away from myself and can't remember the path back

Family; familiar strangers
Look-alikes that reveal a pattern
But, I don't understand the quilt
Can feel them losing softness
Can't blame them
Hard to give comfort
When I'm so uncomfortable giving warmth
They say I'm cold
But I'm left outside always,
Even when they tell me I'm home

What's home, when you can't remember the bed you made?
Or the person next to you...

Eyes that beg for recognition wait for me daily
and I don't remember ever being so scared
Living a horror film
Trying to remember the plot
Hoping there's a happy ending
(How long can my family take the suspense?)

Wish I could act
Kills me the film is running out
and I can't find it;
it's terrifying.

Am I a story meant to be lost?

Vehicle for a Memory

I thought about your red truck today.
The second one,
not the one I remember taking school pics in front of,
back in the 90's,
the newest one.

The one with the pipes on it
that I wish you could push over 90
so we could hear them roar.

I thought I had the coolest grandpa ever
when you pulled up in that truck –
all hipped out,
like you remembered the swag you had
over 60 years ago,
before you became a father and husband.

Running the streets, I imagine,
with the cigars you used to smoke;
One in your mouth
while the wind rippled through your 'fro.
Got Damn!
You were awesome in your glory!

Made everyone laugh until their stomachs
screamed STOP! – they couldn't take it.
I remember you made me laugh so hard
I thought I would piss myself!

You were generations of a soft place to land.
My mother took comfort in your love.
I took comfort in your love.
We all took comfort in your love.

That truck…
That truck was a spaceship
when you were distracted by the TV.
That truck was an ice cream truck
when we trimmed your hedges.
That truck was your second wife,
your mistress,
You loved that truck like it had your rib in it.

That truck…
      Sits in your nephew's yard.
One day it pulled up in the church yard
      and I remember.

I remember the day I stood in your kitchen,
you gazed out the window and vowed:
Soon…
Soon you were fixin' to cruise that truck

You remembered that truck needed its master.
But you forgot
      … that truck was no longer yours.

That you didn't have the power to remember
its functions, let alone your own.
You forgot the controls and your way home,
just the same.

Your brain is a sick thief that
stole your thoughts
      and your identity,
stole your memory
      and your passions.

When I think about the way your mind
turned on you, I see red
brighter than that truck.
I'm stuck between fear and anger.

I'm thankful you haven't forgotten me, but
you've forgotten everything that makes you… you.
And, that's more devastating.

I wonder…
If you saw that truck today, would it trigger a memory?
Would it pop the trunk that holds your glorious past?
Or have you forgotten that? – like the reflection you'd see
in its rearview.

Grandpa's Mind

One time, I asked you a question.

In your muddy brown eyes,
I watched you trudge through your mind
and dig through answers,
watched you suffer, trying to move
your feet through your thoughts.
Seemed like forever,
before I pulled you out of that
secluded place of confusion
by changing the subject,
replacing the page of conversation.

My heart shreds
at every moment I remember
all you've forgotten.

You still smile the same.
Your heart's still the same.
But, you speak like someone changed your voice box.
Randomly, you say things you wouldn't be caught dead saying.
Your lips and tongue were saturated in respect.
Yet, sometimes, in your eyes, I see
your mind and soul don't connect.

And I can't find you in those dusty windows.

When I visit, I always leave happy
that at least you know exactly who I am.
I love when you ask me
how my daughter is doing.

I just hate when you ask me, every day,
what her name is.

You started forgetting your way home.
The simplest route has been distorted.
You can't picture the way back
to the place you love most.
Although, your chair is always waiting,
the chair you slept snoring in
more often than your own bed.

We stood, looking out your window, talking
and I didn't mean to ignore what you were saying.
I just felt guilty.

I was glad you forgot
               … that we took your truck from you.

I miss the days that truck was a playground.
You would rarely yell, but it pissed you off
when we monkeyed around on the side railings.
Especially, when you needed to focus on the path ahead.

I wish you remembered the days it was
our ice cream truck without the jingle.
Or the sweet sounds of a brown bag
full of 25 cent creamsicles;
cold edible currency you paid us
every time we helped you in the yard.

Now, I'd give anything for you to remember the seasons.
So that you wouldn't walk outside in your jacket
in the middle of summer.
Or come inside and turn your stove on high
so that, in the middle of winter,

you wouldn't reach above your head and
blast frigid air through your wrinkled skin.

It saddens me that you can't remember
What time it is,
What day it is,
Or your mother.

It dangles me over despair that you've forgotten her.
She was your favorite person,
and you couldn't tell me her name.
You once played back full conversations you had with her,
but now can't describe what she looked like,
the lessons she taught you,
how she raised all six of your kids –
my mother being your first.
I'm glad you remember her.
You always remember to tell me to thank her
when I drop off meals she prepares for you;
made with my mother's love,
carried by my tired, fearful feet.

Hoping today isn't the day you ask,
Who...
      ... *I* am.

Remembering Mortality

You grab my face and force me to stare mortality in the eyes force me to acknowledge the force of my fear,

how finite my tomorrows are, how small my sorrows are.

You forgot me.
                        You forgot yourself.
It wasn't your fault.
                        Your brain broke itself.

You are the reflection of my worst nightmares.

Deterioration, without knowledge of it,
Stuck in an infinite loop of forgetfulness,
You don't even realize you're alive.

I wonder
What's the price of such ignorant bliss?
Would death finding you be more glorious than
                        This life of emptiness?

I run from your expressionless face,
                        Your backspacing mind,
and hide from your presence,
for as long as I can disguise
                        the disappearing act
I'm running out of diversions.
My guilt is grabbing me by the throat,
                        squeezing harder each day;

Because my mother can't do the same,
can't pretend her father doesn't exist.

I must have forgotten...
I don't get to monopolize this
                    pain we all feel.

5
to live beyond death

Immortality

I'm not afraid of dying ... anymore. But they say when no one is left to remember you that you die twice. What terrifies me is that one day, no one will know I once walked this earth, that I gave effort in this thing we call life. That my existence wasn't for nothing.

I became an artist. Like most artists, I believe our intention is for our art to live on long after we are gone. I believe that is, so we never truly die but live on through our works. If my memory fades and I cease to remember who I am, when my eyes close for the last time and I take my last breath and exhale, I hope my poetry will live on.

I hope my words will keep the memory of me warm in someone's heart. That my name will travel off someone's lips. Through my creativity, I seek to become immortal.

Content

I hope to never be a short story.

These days I make content
to make sure I'm not forgotten, like the contents
of Grandma and Grandpa's house.
Hope my verses move in
like Kiana did to their place,
refresh themselves;
bad memories fought to be replaced.
Good memories I try to replay
before my tape runs out.

I can't remember the words my Poppa said,
but I know he gave me gems.
My Grandma was a diamond,
but we didn't love her like him.
They say diamonds are forever, though,
and I remember her more.
Words she said burn through my head;
I'm afraid they'll be ash and buried
like the corpse I'll leave.

So, I mine my words to embed
to ensure I'm never dead.
I hope I leave a good story,
live real enough to be non-fiction,
the Creator's creative creation.
My pen builds a world I can't be forgotten in,
poetic devices the on switch to memories
when my light turns out.

Hope the stage will hold a memory
of when I talked them out of darkness,
even when my own shadow choked me.

I can be content with taking my last breath
as long as my content outlasts death.

Remember Me

Who will remember me?
Will I fade, like endings to songs?

Used to curse the day I was born,
but now care more that I'm not forgotten.
(probably my biggest secret)
Funny, the mask of pride enables me to hide.
I'll swear I'm OK,
and you'll see that as truth.
I'll walk away
and ask myself if I lied.
So, please…

Remember
the smiles we share,
and the laughter during our days;
the way I treasure the ones
that made me double over
in the sweet pain
of Happiness in my ribcage.

Remember
life is dramatic and funny
in dark ways, but still full of light.
Life is more sunshine than gloom.

Remember
When times are hard, all the answers
and escape to eternal freedom
may be just another tear away
… or another smile.

Remember
When I make it to the glorious place,
when my spirit tears my flesh and flies away,
I wish to be a memory which never fades,
to be the thought that keeps someone warm
in the chill of their winter days.

Remember me.
           Remember me.

Colophon

Wider Perspectives Publishing regrets to have to announce that the ongoing Colophon page, used to tout artists published in books from WPP, has to be reworked. This is due to the growing library of fine writers coming out of, or even into, the Hampton Roads area of Virginia.

Jason Brown (Drk Mtr)
Ken Sutton
Kailyn Rae Sasso
Crickyt J. ExpressionSamantha Casey
Donna Burnett-Robinson
Se'Mon-Michelle Rosser
Lisa M. Kendrick
Cassandra IsFree
Nich (Nicholis Williams)
Samantha Geovjian Clarke
Natalie Morison-Uzzle
Gus Woodward II
Patsy Bickerstaff
Edith Blake
Jack Cassada
Dezz
Daniel Garwood
Jada Hollingsworth
Tabetha Moon House
Nick Marickovich
Grey Hues
Rivers Raye
Madeline Garcia
Chichi Iwuorie
Symay Rhodes
Arlandria Speaks (Faith Clay)
Terra Leigh
Raymond M. Simmons
Samantha Borders-Shoemaker
Taz Weysweete'
Jade Leonard

Darean Polk
Bobby K.
    (The Poor Man's Poet)
Faith Griffin
J. Scott Wilson (Teech!)
Charles Wilson
Gloria Darlene Mann
Neil Spirtas
Jorge Mendez & JT Williams
Sarah Eileen Williams
Stephanie Diana (Noftz)
Shanya – Lady S.

Crystal Nolen
Catherine TL Hodges
Kent Knowlton
Linda Spence-Howard
Tony Broadway
Zach Crowe

Maria April C.
Mark Willoughby
Martina Champion
… and others to come soon.

the Hampton Roads
  Artistic Collective (757
  Perspectives) &
The Poet's Domain
are all WPP literary journals in cooperation with Scientific Eve or Live Wire Press

Check for those artists on FaceBook, Instagram, the Virginia Poetry Online channel on YouTube, and other social media.

Chris The Poetic Genius Green

www.ingramcontent.com/pod-product-compliance
Lightning Source LLC
Chambersburg PA
CBHW060035180426

43196CB00045B/2689